TIMELINES OF
AMERICAN HISTORY™

A Timeline of Congress

Lisa Modifica

rosen central™

The Rosen Publishing Group, Inc., New York

Published in 2004 by The Rosen Publishing Group, Inc.
29 East 21st Street, New York, NY 10010

Copyright © 2004 by The Rosen Publishing Group, Inc.

First Edition

Library of Congress Cataloging-in-Publication Data

Modifica, Lisa.
A timeline of Congress / Lisa Modifica.
    p. cm.—(Timelines of American history)
Summary: Provides a chronological look at the history of the United States Congress and at the legislators who have made their mark there.
Includes bibliographical references (p.   ) and index.
ISBN 0-8239-4534-0 (lib. bdg.)
1. United States. Congress—History—Chronology—Juvenile literature. 2. Legislators—United States—History—Juvenile literature. [1. United States. Congress—History—Chronology. 2. Legislators—History.] I. Title. II. Series.
JK1025.M63 2003
328.73'002'02—dc22

2003016007

Manufactured in the United States of America

On the cover: A meeting of American congressmen. Painting by Ernest Clifford Piexotto.
On the title page: Signatures on the last page of the Olive Branch petition sent by individual members of the First Continental Congress in Philadelphia to King George.

Contents

1

The Beginning

There are two branches of Congress. The Senate is one branch. The Senate is made up of two senators from each state. The other branch is called the House of Representatives. The number of representatives for each state depends on how many people live there. Bigger states have more representatives. Altogether, there are 435 representatives in the House of Representatives. Senators and representatives make decisions for the people who live in their states. People vote for who they want to represent them in each branch of Congress.

The United States Capitol Complex—which is the national government center—includes the Capitol (shown here in the spring), congressional office buildings, the Library of Congress buildings, the Supreme Court Building, the U.S. Botanic Garden, the Capitol Power Plant, and other facilities.

1787
The Founding Fathers writing the United States Constitution create Congress as one of the three branches of government.

1789
Congress meets for the first time in New York.

1790
Congress begins meeting in Philadelphia. They meet there while the new capital is being planned in Washington, D.C.

1792
The United States government announces a contest to design the Capitol. None of the plans submitted are satisfactory.

July 25, 1793
President George Washington approves the proposed design of Dr. William Thornton, who had been allowed to submit his design after the competition was over.

September 18, 1793
President Washington lays the cornerstone of the building's southeast corner and construction begins.

1794
For the first time, the Senate refuses to allow an elected representative to serve, Albert Gallatin of Pennsylvania, because some senators say he has not been an American citizen long enough. Gallatin becomes a member of the House of Representatives in 1795.

What Congress Does

Congress makes federal laws about all kinds of issues. Federal laws affect the whole country. Congress is the part of the American government that spends the money that people pay in taxes. It also decides how much people pay in taxes. As well, Congress makes laws about immigration, civil rights, the mail, drugs, television, the space program, airlines, and lots of other things. Congress controls many of the actions of the president. If the president wants to make a law or spend money, he must first ask Congress.

★ **1795**
The Senate allows the public to watch its sessions. (Today, the public is still allowed to attend the Senate's sessions.) For the first time, the Senate rejects a Supreme Court nominee—John Rutledge. Rutledge was against Jay's Treaty, a trade agreement with Great Britain.

★ **1798**
The Senate holds its first impeachment trial to decide if Senator William Blount of Tennessee should be impeached.

★ **1800**
The Senate moves from Philadelphia to the north wing of the unfinished Capitol in Washington, D.C.

This is one of architect Benjamin Henry Latrobe's blueprints of the north wing of the United States Capitol. Latrobe drew this in 1814. Blueprints used to be printed with special blue ink—thus, the name. The Capitol was under construction from 1793 to 1830.

1802 ★

For the first time, official note takers are allowed in the Senate chamber.

1803 ★

Benjamin Henry Latrobe, an Englishman, takes over construction of the Capitol. Latrobe moved to America in 1795.

The Speaker of the House

The Speaker of the House becomes president if something happens to the president and the vice president. The Speaker of the House is the leader of the House of Representatives from the majority party at that time. The Speaker is in charge of selecting who speaks in the House of Representatives. Before 1910, the Speaker also selected the leaders of each committee. Committees are groups that are formed

The current Speaker of the House, Dennis Hastert, speaks at his office in Batavia, Illinois, one week before he is elected as Speaker of the House in 1999. The Speaker of the House is the third highest elected official in the U.S. government. Speaker Hastert is now serving his third term as Speaker and his ninth term as the Republican congressman for Illinois's 14th Congressional District.

to work on a bill when it comes to Congress. Committees debate a bill, change it, and then reintroduce it to the House or Senate.

★ **1804**
The Senate convicts federal judge John Pickering of misconduct and removes him from office. It is the first time there is a conviction following an impeachment trial.

★ **1805**
Vice President Aaron Burr resigns after shooting Alexander Hamilton in a duel that took place on July 11, 1804, in Weehawken, New Jersey.

★ **1807**
The House of Representatives moves into the south wing of the Capitol.

Henry Clay

★ **1811**
Representative Henry Clay becomes Speaker of the House. He is the first Speaker to use his position in debates and for control of the floor. He earns the nickname "the Great Compromiser" because he helps parties in Congress settle arguments and pass bills.

2

Race and Slavery in Congress

During the 1800s, Congress was split over the issues of secession and slavery. Many members of Congress wanted to keep the Union together, which meant allowing slavery in the South. Many other senators and representatives wanted to abolish slavery in the whole country. Northern members of Congress would only admit

This image shows a white landowner overseeing a group of black cotton pickers in Texas around 1800. Cotton was first grown in Texas by Spanish missionaries. Cotton that was planted in the spring was harvested and handpicked in late August. Of the estimated 212,592 people in Texas in 1850, 27.4 percent—or 58,161—were slaves.

Missouri as a slave state after Maine was admitted as a state without slavery. This kept an equal amount of nonslave and slave states in the Union. Missouri also had to promise that free blacks could move there.

★ **1814**
The British set fire to the Capitol and other buildings in Washington, D.C.

Fire at the Capitol

★ **1818**
John H. Eaton becomes a senator even though he is only twenty-eight years old. There is a rule that all senators must be at least thirty. Charles Bulfinch takes over restoration of the Capitol. Construction on the central building begins.

★ **1819**
The Senate and the House of Representatives begin to meet in the Capitol again.

★ **1820**
After much discussion and argument, Congress agrees to the Missouri Compromise. The Missouri Compromise is a complicated bill that admits Missouri to the Union as a slave state. Representative Henry Clay works very hard to reach a compromise and avoid war.

11

The Shape of Congress

The people who work in Congress make decisions for all the people who live in the states they represent. Members of Congress decide who has certain rights or when something is unfair. They know what the people in their states want, and they vote for it. Members of Congress must be diverse so that all Americans feel they are being represented in their government.

A view of the Lower House—the House of Representatives—in 1866. The Upper House is the Senate. These houses are both part of Congress. This is known as the bicameral system, and it dates back to seventeenth-century England.

1829

The Capitol is completed, and the grounds surrounding it are landscaped.

1841

The Senate begins its use of filibusters. A filibuster is when a congressperson speaks for a long time about one subject to delay a vote. Representatives or senators of the minority party often use filibusters when the majority is about to pass a bill. The first filibuster lasted approximately eighteen days.

1845

David Levy Yulee becomes the first Jewish senator.

Congress decides that the first Tuesday after the first Monday in November will be Election Day.

1846

Members of the same party begin to sit together in the Senate.

This portrait of the Honorable David Levy Yulee was taken around 1855. Yulee was born in the U.S. Virgin Islands in 1811. In 1839, Yulee helped write Florida's constitution and was sent as a territorial delegate to the United States Congress. When Florida became a state in 1845, he was elected as one of the two senators from Florida.

Compromise of 1850

In 1848, the Mexican-American War ended, and the United States had to decide if the territory it won would allow slavery. Northerners did not want slavery, and Southerners said if the territory did not allow slaves, they would secede. California also wanted to be admitted as a free state. Henry Clay and Stephen A. Douglas helped to create a series of bills about the territories. Some states came in as free states, some allowed slaves, and some states were allowed to

Henry Clay addresses the United States Senate in 1850. Clay, who was born on April 12, 1777, in Hanover County, Virginia, was secretary of state under John Quincy Adams. He was an unsuccessful candidate for the presidency in 1824, 1832, and 1844.

decide if they wanted slavery. This important compromise delayed war in America for another decade.

★ **1849**

California asks to be admitted to the Union as a free state.

★ **1850**

The Compromise of 1850 is reached. Senator Daniel Webster gives a famous speech in the Senate. He wants Northerners to be tolerant of slavery in the South in order to keep the Union together.

Senator Daniel Webster

A contest is held for designs to enlarge the Capitol. Congress is not able to decide between two designs. The $500 prize money is divided among five architects, and it becomes President Millard Fillmore's job to choose a plan and appoint an architect. He decides on the plan by Thomas U. Walter.

★ **1857**

The House of Representatives begins to meet in a new hall in the Capitol.

★ **1859**

The Senate begins to meet in a new chamber in the Capitol. Senator David Broderick becomes the only senator to die in a duel.

3

Changes in Congress

Andrew Johnson became president when Abraham Lincoln was assassinated in 1865. At the time, Reconstruction was going on, and there were many members of Congress who disagreed with many of Johnson's ideas. Johnson broke a congressional law. Even though he had only a few months left to serve as president, Congress began the process of impeachment. Eventually, the attempt at impeachment failed, and Johnson was allowed to finish his term.

An admission ticket to the impeachment trial of President Andrew Johnson. This impeachment trial judged whether President Johnson should be removed from office. Johnson, who was born in Raleigh, North Carolina, had been elected to Congress in 1843.

1861

On January 21, Jefferson Davis delivers a farewell speech to the Senate. He is leaving to become president of the Confederacy.

During the Civil War, the Capitol is used as a bakery, hospital, and place to sleep.

1863

The *Statue of Freedom*, designed by Thomas Crawford, is put on the top of the Capitol dome.

1868

President Johnson replaces Secretary of War Edwin Stanton even though he needs Congress's approval to do so. In doing this, he has broken a law called the Tenure of Office Act.

March 23, 1868

The impeachment trial of President Andrew Johnson begins in the Senate. It is the first time that Congress tries to impeach a president. In the end, the Senate is one vote short of impeaching Johnson.

1870

Hiram Revels of Adams County, Mississippi, becomes the first black senator.

On February 25, 1870, Senator Hiram Revels takes the oath of office in Washington, D.C. Revels was born in 1822 in Fayetteville, North Carolina.

Democracy in Congress

In 1913, the Constitution was changed so voters could elect their own senators. Before 1913, senators were elected by state legislature. Each state is divided into sections called congressional districts. Each congressional district has about the same amount of people living in it. A census is taken during the first year of each decade, and districts are changed based on population. Each congressional district elects a representative to the House. The population of a state only matters in the House of Representatives.

Passengers riding on the U.S. Senate subway on March 23, 1922. The subway system shuttles senators and others between the U.S. Capitol and the Senate office buildings. In 1961, a modern subway was installed that cost between $12 million and $18 million.

1875
Andrew Johnson becomes the first former president to become a senator.

1890
Workers install electric lights throughout the Capitol.

1894
Modern plumbing is installed throughout the Capitol.

1906
To make travel easier, Congress authorizes funds to build a subway between the Capitol and the Senate office building. It was first used in 1909.

1907
Charles Curtis of Kansas becomes the first senator from India.

Senator
Charles Curtis

1910
Representatives feel Speaker Joseph G. Cannon is abusing his power. They give him a less important position.

The Speaker of the House no longer chooses committee leaders or members.

1913
The Constitution is amended so the public can elect senators directly. The House of Representatives limits the number of representatives to 435. Before 1913, the number of representatives increased as the population grew.

Women in Congress

In 1916, Jeannette Rankin was the first woman to be elected to the House of Representatives. Women were not granted the right to vote until 1920. It is amazing that Rankin was elected before she was allowed to vote! Fourteen years after Rankin lost her bid for senator, Hattie Ophelia Wyatt Caraway became the first woman elected to the Senate.

★ **1917**
Filibusters are still allowed in the Senate. The House of Representatives creates a rule to limit filibusters. Because the House is so large, representatives are not allowed to speak for an unlimited time.

★ **1916**
Jeannette Rankin is elected to the House of Representatives. She was known for her position against the United States's participation in World War I and World War II.

★ **1918**
Jeannette Rankin is the first woman to run for a seat in the Senate. She loses.

★ **1920**
Warren G. Harding is the first man to become president while serving as a senator.

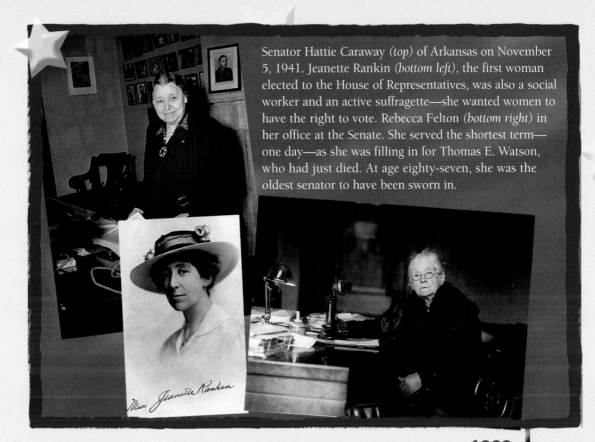

Senator Hattie Caraway *(top)* of Arkansas on November 5, 1941. Jeanette Rankin *(bottom left)*, the first woman elected to the House of Representatives, was also a social worker and an active suffragette—she wanted women to have the right to vote. Rebecca Felton *(bottom right)* in her office at the Senate. She served the shortest term—one day—as she was filling in for Thomas E. Watson, who had just died. At age eighty-seven, she was the oldest senator to have been sworn in.

1922 ★

Rebecca Felton is the first woman appointed to the senate, but she serves for only twenty-four hours. She is appointed when Senator Thomas E. Watson dies, and she is removed when a replacement for Watson is appointed.

1928 ★

Octaviano Larrazolo becomes the first Latino senator to serve in Congress.

1932 ★

Hattie Ophelia Wyatt Caraway is the first woman elected to the Senate.

4

The New Congress

The U.S. Army–McCarthy congressional hearings were held and televised from April to June 1954. A member of Senator Joseph R. McCarthy's staff was drafted into the army, and the senator tried to pressure the army into giving the staff member special privileges. When army officials became angry with McCarthy, he accused them of hiding Communists within their organization. Then Senator McCarthy widened his attacks and began accusing many organizations and people of being Communists.

★ **1939**
The Senate passes a rule that each day's session will open with a prayer.

★ **1946**
President Harry S. Truman signs an act that creates an organized staff system for Congress. Because of this act, members of Congress hire their own staff.

★ **1949**
The chambers of the House of Representatives and Senate are remodeled.

Senator Joseph McCarthy *(left)* and Roy Cohn (to Senator McCarthy's left) listen to the testimony of Army Secretary Robert Stevens at the Senate investigating subcommittee hearing.

1954 ★

The Senate begins the U.S. Army–McCarthy hearings, which are televised. For many Americans, this is the first time they see a congressional hearing. The hearings last thirty-six days. McCarthy thinks there are many Communists in the United States. He unfairly accuses many Americans of being Communists. His political position suffers because of the hearings.

1958 ★

The Senate opens its second office building.

1959 ★

Hiram L. Fong becomes the first Chinese American senator.

23

Too Much Power for the President

The Watergate investigation began when men were arrested for breaking into the offices of the Democratic National Committee in 1972. The five men caught had ties to President Richard Nixon. After investigating the president, Congress discovered that Nixon had done many illegal things. The Watergate investigation showed that the president had gained too much power in the government. Congress was able to take back some power after Nixon resigned.

After resigning as president, Richard Nixon speaks at the White House. With him are his family: from left, son-in-law David Eisenhower; daughter Julie Nixon-Eisenhower; wife Pat Nixon; and daughter Tricia Nixon, with her husband, Edward Cox.

1974

President Richard M. Nixon resigns after Congress proves he has been acting illegally. He had used money given to him illegally and hired the men that broke into the headquarters of the Democratic National Committee. People working for Nixon also forged signatures and taped phone calls to embarrass politicians who were running against him. Nixon knew he would probably be impeached if a trial began.

1975

The Senate allows the public to attend committee meetings.

1979

The cable channel C-Span begins to show the House of Representatives on television every day.

1982

The Senate opens its third office building.

1986

The cable television channel C-Span 2 begins to show the Senate on television every day.

1988

Representatives begin to say the Pledge of Allegiance at the beginning of every session.

1993

Carol Moseley Braun is the first black woman to become a senator.

Congress Today

Today, Congress still works much the same as it did when it was created. Both the Senate and the House of Representatives are very important parts of the government. They make sure that the president is not abusing his power. Congress is part of the system of checks and balances that helps the government work. Congress also makes important decisions about many issues in the United States. Because the United States is a democracy, voters get to choose who serves in Congress.

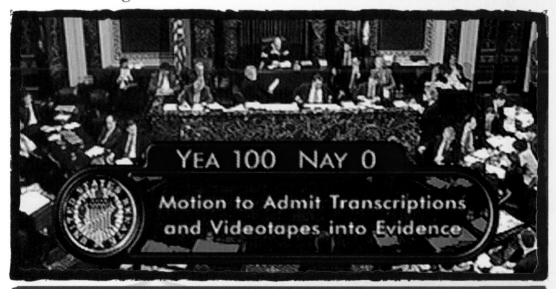

During the impeachment trial of President Clinton, a vote was taken to decide whether transcripts and videotapes from the deposition of three witnesses were to be admitted as evidence. The video screen pictured here shows the results of the vote—100 to 0. This took place in Washington, D.C., on February 4, 1999.

1999
The Senate holds the impeachment trial of President Bill Clinton. This is the second impeachment trial of a president.

2000
Hillary Rodham Clinton is the first former first lady to become a senator.

First Lady and senator-elect Hillary Rodham Clinton addresses supporters during her victory rally in New York on Tuesday, November 7, 2000. Clinton was the first wife of a president to be elected to Congress.

2001
On September 11, there are terrorist attacks on the World Trade Center and the Pentagon. Members of Congress are forced to leave the Capitol and Senate office buildings.

2002
Senator Frank Murkowski resigns to become the governor of Alaska. He appoints his daughter, Lisa Murkowski, to fill his position. This is the first time a father and his daughter have served as senators.

Lisa Murkowski is sworn in as senator.

Timelines Make Learning Fun

A timeline is a way for us to learn about history. A timeline lists important events and gives the year or date that they happened. Using basic math, you can see how much time passed before other events happened. Timelines are also a quick way to find out a lot of information about one subject. Think about what you would put on a timeline of your life. You would probably put when you were born, when you went to school, and when your siblings were born. A reader would quickly learn a lot about you.

Glossary

amend (uh-MEND) To change something for the better.

compromise (KOM-pruh-myz) When two people or parties each change how they feel a little bit so they can agree.

Confederacy (kun-FEH-duh-reh-see) The eleven Southern states that declared themselves separate from the United States in 1860 and 1861.

congressional (kon-GRESH-un-al) Relating to Congress.

federal (FEH-duh-rul) Something relating to the whole country.

filibuster (FIH-li-bus-tur) When a member of Congress speaks for a long time about one subject to delay a vote.

House of Representatives (HOWS UV reh-prih-ZEN-tuh-tivs) One of the two branches of Congress.

impeach (im-PEECH) To charge someone with a crime.

investigation (in-veh-stih-GAY-shun) The act of examining something or someone.

landscape (LAND-skayp) To arrange and plan land.

legislature (LEH-jis-lay-chur) A group of people who can make laws.

majority (muh-JOR-ih-tee) The larger part of a group.

minority (my-NOR-ih-tee) The lesser part of a group.

nominee (nah-mih-NEE) Someone who is chosen for a position.

privileges (PRIV-lij-ez) Special benefits given to someone.

Reconstruction (ree-kun-STRUK-shun) A period of time, from 1865 to 1877, after the Civil War when the federal government controlled Southern states before they were allowed to join the Union again.

represent (reh-prih-ZENT) To speak for someone.

restoration (reh-stuh-RAY-shun) Making something like it was before.

secession (sih-CES-shun) Leaving membership of a group. The South seceded from the United States before the Civil War.

Senate (SEH-nit) One of the two branches of Congress.

session (SEH-shun) A meeting.

tolerant (TAH-ler-ent) Allowing others to have opinions different from yours.

Web Sites

Due to the changing nature of Internet links, the Rosen Publishing Group, Inc., has developed an online list of Web sites related to the subject of this book. This site is updated regularly. Please use this link to access the list:

http://www.rosenlinks.com/ntk/tah/cong

Index

A Timeline of Congress

Credits

About the author: Lisa Modifica is a freelance writer.

Photo credits: Cover © Geoffrey Clements/Corbis; pp. 1, 10, 12, 15 © Hulton Archive/ Getty Images; p. 4 © Alan Schein Photography/Corbis; pp. 7, 18, 21 (bottom right) © Corbis; pp. 8, 24, 26, 27 (top and bottom) AP/Wide World Photos; pp. 9, 16, 21 (top left), 23 © Bettmann/Corbis; pp. 11, 13, 14, 19, 21 (bottom left) © Library of Congress Prints and Photographs Division; p. 17 (top) © Theodore Horydczak Collection/Library of Congress.

Designer: Geri Fletcher; Editor: Annie Sommers